Contents

KU-484-339

You can find words in bold, **like this**, in the Glossary.

Weather

Are you interested in the weather? Have you ever tried to guess what it is going to be like? It is actually very difficult to predict! In this book, you can find out how professionals try to forecast the weather. It will also give you ideas about what you can try to forecast and how you should do it. In the other books in this series, you can find out more about each type of weather, and how you can use simple apparatus to help measure the weather.

Forecasting the weather has always been an interesting thing to do. With some knowledge and simple apparatus, you can make your own reasonable predictions about the weather. By watching the weather carefully, you can collect **data**, and then see if there are any patterns in this data. If you collect similar data in the future, this might help you to tell what the coming weather is going to be like.

It is the change in weather in the different seasons that triggers when trees and other plants grow and then shed their leaves. Farmers grow food according to these seasons. Predicting unexpected weather can stop crops being ruined.

FORECASTING
THE WEATHER

REVISED AND UPDATED

Measuring the Weather

Alan Rodgers and Angella Streluk

www.heinemann.co.uk/library
Visit our website to find out more information about Heinemann Library books.

To order:
☎ Phone 44 (0) 1865 888066
🖹 Send a fax to 44 (0)1865 314091
🖥 Visit the Heinemann Library Bookshop at www.heinemann.co.uk/library to browse our catalogue and order online.

First published in Great Britain by Heinemann Library, Halley Court, Jordan Hill, Oxford OX2 8EJ, part of Harcourt Education.
Heinemann Library is a registered trademark of Harcourt Education Ltd.

© Harcourt Education Ltd 2008
The moral right of the proprietor has been asserted.

All rights reserved. No part of this publication may be reproduced, stored in a retrieval system, or transmitted in any form or by any means, electronic, mechanical, photocopying, recording, or otherwise, without either the prior written permission of the publishers or a licence permitting restricted copying in the United Kingdom issued by the Copyright Licensing Agency Ltd, 90 Tottenham Court Road, London W1T 4LP (www.cla.co.uk).

Editorial: Joanna Talbot
Design: Michelle Lisseter and Philippa Jenkins
Picture Research: Ruth Blair
Production: Julie Carter

Originated by Chroma Graphics
Printed and bound in China by South China Printing Company Limited

ISBN 978 0 431 03856 8
12 11 10 09 08
10 9 8 7 6 5 4 3 2 1

British Library Cataloguing in Publication Data
Rodgers, Alan
    Forecasting the weather. - (Measuring the weather)
    1. Weather forecasting - Juvenile literature
    I. Title II. Streluk, Angella
    5 5 1.6'3
A full catalogue record for this book is available from the British Library.

Acknowledgements
The Publishers would like to thank the following for permission to reproduce photographs: Bruce Coleman Collection pp. **17**, **18**; Camera Press p. **29**; FLPA p. **8**; Fotomas Index p. **22**; OSF p. **27**; Photodisc p. **26**; Robert Harding Picture Library pp. **19**, **29**; Science Photo Library pp. **4**, **6**, **23**, **24**; Trevor Clifford Photography pp. **7**, **9**, **12**, **13**, **20**; www.wunderground.com/ p. **25**.

Cover images reproduced with permission of Jeff Edwards and Science Photo Library.

Our thanks to Jacquie Syvret of the Met Office for her assistance during the preparation of this book.

Every effort has been made to contact copyright holders of any material reproduced in this book. Any omissions will be rectified in subsequent printings if notice is given to the publishers.

Disclaimer
All the Internet addresses (URLs) given in this book were valid at the time of going to press. However, due to the dynamic nature of the Internet, some addresses may have changed, or sites may have changed or ceased to exist since publication. While the author and publishers regret any inconvenience this may cause readers, no responsibility for any such changes can be accepted by either the author or publishers.

ROTHERHAM LIBRARY & INFORMATION SERVICES	
B49 046191 3	
Askews	
J551.63	£11.99

We have all seen weather forecasts on television or in newspapers. These forecasts use simple picture symbols to represent the weather, so that it is easy to work out what they mean. But the symbols used by professional weather forecasters are very different. **Meteorologists** who study the weather around the world all use the same symbols, so that they can exchange information.

Weather all over the world

Although people are most interested in the weather where they are, it is really a global interest. This is because the Sun affects all parts of the Earth. The movement of the Earth causes day and night, which causes changes in temperature. The tilt of the Earth gives us seasons. This means that different parts of the Earth are heated at different times. This heat, or the lack of it, produces the weather.

The study of climate is also very important. Climate is the long-term weather over a number of years. Monitoring the climate helps meteorologists to spot if there are changes in things such as temperature over a long period of time.

Be careful!

Do not look directly at the Sun when studying the weather. Never shelter under trees during a thunderstorm, as they may be hit by lightning.

*These are just some of the symbols used by professional meteorologists. They include symbols for cloud cover, **precipitation** (such as rain and snow), and wind speed.*

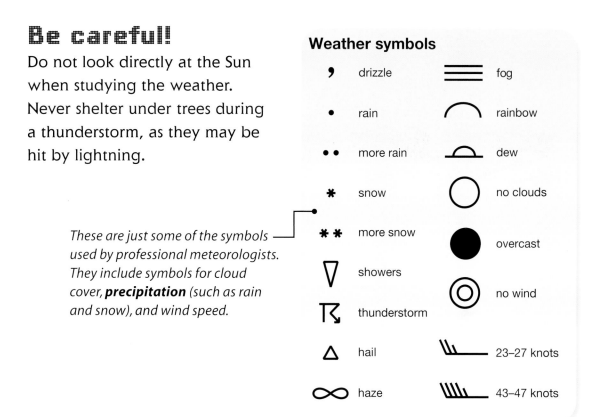

Weather symbols

,	drizzle	☰	fog
•	rain	⌒	rainbow
• •	more rain	⌂	dew
✳	snow	○	no clouds
✳ ✳	more snow	●	overcast
▽	showers	◎	no wind
⚡	thunderstorm		
△	hail	⚞—	23–27 knots
∞	haze	⚟—	43–47 knots

What is a weather station?

To record weather **data**, certain instruments are needed. These are often kept in the same location, and make up what is called a **weather station**. A weather station's main instruments are stored inside a special box called a Stevenson Screen. This was invented by Thomas Stevenson. A Stevenson Screen is a white rainproof box with a door. The sides are made from slats that allow air to move around inside the box, but do not create draughts or let in rain. The door should face north if you live north of the equator, or south if you live south of the equator. This means that when the door is opened, the Sun will not shine on the instruments and affect their readings. Smaller, less expensive Stevenson Screen kits are available for use by amateurs.

Several instruments are needed to record basic weather data. The best results will be obtained from the most expensive equipment that can be bought. However, good results can also be gained from quite cheap instruments.

Because a Stevenson Screen is white, it reflects the sunlight. The instruments for recording the weather will then not be affected by direct sunlight or draughts. This picture shows a Stevenson Screen with its door open.

Instruments for running a weather station

Thermometers are kept in the Stevenson Screen. They are used for measuring temperatures. A maximum and minimum thermometer records the highest and lowest temperatures over a period of time. A wet and dry bulb **hygrometer** helps you to work out how much moisture (**humidity**) is in the air. All of these readings can also be recorded by an inexpensive digital instrument. A wind vane is used to show the wind direction. Rain gauges record how much rain has fallen. A **barometer**, which can be kept indoors, measures **air pressure**.

The next most useful addition to a weather station is a grass minimum thermometer, which is used to measure the temperature at ground level. You could use an ordinary maximum and minimum thermometer, placed just above some short grass near the Stevenson Screen. Another good instrument to have is a soil thermometer, which measures the temperature in the ground. If possible, have two of these, of different lengths.

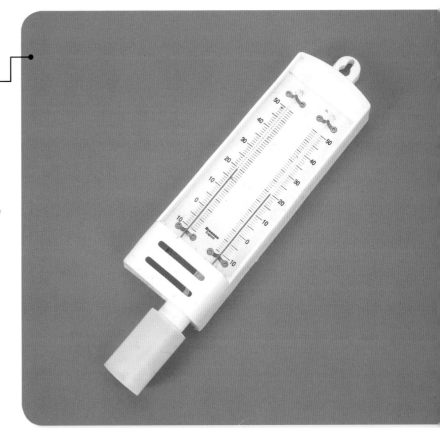

*This wet and dry bulb hygrometer has two thermometers. One thermometer has its **bulb** wrapped in a wet **wick**. This thermometer always has its temperature reduced by the **evaporation** of the water in the wick. The readings from the two thermometers are compared to calculate the **relative humidity**.*

Where to place a weather station

Meteorologists all position their weather instruments in a standard way, so that **data** can be shared and compared. They give exact details about the location of their **weather stations**, including the height above sea level. This information helps meteorologists to understand the difference made to weather data by various locations.

Your weather station should be placed on level ground that is covered in short grass. It should be well away from large obstacles, like trees or walls. The Stevenson Screen should be set firmly on a stand, so that the instruments are at a height of 1.25 metres (4.1 feet) above the ground.

Measuring the weather

To find out the wind direction, you need a **weather vane**. It should be placed well away from obstacles that would prevent the wind from directing its pointer. It is best if the weather vane is two to four times the height of the nearest obstacle. To measure the strength of the wind, stand where you can see things blowing about. Then use the **Beaufort scale** (see page 11) to estimate the wind's strength.

Weather instruments are kept close together, so that their readings are all from the same location.

Clouds and rainfall

Knowing what types of clouds are in the sky will help with your forecast. Stand where you can clearly see the sky to look at a cloud type and the amount of this cloud in the sky. When you are measuring the weather, never look directly at the Sun. It can damage your eyes.

To measure rainfall, use a rain gauge. It should be sited well away from tall objects so that it is not sheltered from the rain. The rim of the funnel should be 305 millimetres (12 inches) above the ground. This is so rain does not splash up from the surface and give false readings. The diameter of the funnel should be 127 millimetres (5 inches).

Thermometers

Some thermometers should be placed outside the Stevenson Screen. Grass minimum thermometers are used to measure the lowest temperature on the ground. They need to be set in an open space, just above the level of short grass. Soil thermometers measure the temperature below the surface of the ground. They should be set into the ground inside a hollow steel tube. Any snow that falls near them should be cleared away, because it can affect the thermometer's reading.

Grass minimum thermometers (shown at the bottom of the picture) can be expensive, but are very accurate instruments. An inexpensive alternative is an ordinary maximum and minimum thermometer, shown at the top.

Recording weather data

It is important to collect weather **data** regularly. This means that patterns in the weather can be spotted. Even with simple instruments, useful data can be collected. Don't worry if you do not have an ideal place to set up your instruments. It is better to collect any data than no data! Record the data on a sheet labelled with the date and where the data is from. If someone is interested in your data, this information will help them to understand it.

TRY THIS YOURSELF!

Here are some things to record when you are collecting weather data:

- Maximum temperature – record the highest temperature for the previous 24 hours
- Minimum temperature – record the lowest temperature for the previous 24 hours
- **Dry temperature** – record the current temperature
- **Wet temperature** – record the temperature on the special thermometer to find the amount of water in the air. Check there is water in the container that keeps the wick wet.
- **Relative humidity** – calculate this as a percentage from a set of wet and dry temperatures
- Pressure – read in millibars or kiloPascals from a barometer
- Wind direction – record which way the wind is blowing from
- Wind strength – look at the trees and other movable items and assess the number on the **Beaufort scale**
- Cloud amount – record the amount of cloud cover by dividing the sky into eight parts. The official term is **oktas**. If the sky is completely cloudy, your reading will be eight. If the clouds cover half of the sky, record it as four oktas.
- Cloud type – record the main cloud type for the sky. See page 15 for the names of some of the clouds.
- Rain – record the contents of the rain gauge in millimetres or inches and then empty it

The best time to record data is at 9:00 a.m. ,which is the time that many other weather stations record their data. Your data could then be compared with theirs.

Date	Day	Max. temp.	Min temp.	Dry temp.	Wet temp.	Relative humidity	Pressure	Wind direction	Wind strength	Cloud amount	Cloud type	Rain	Present
1	M	11.6	5.6	6.4	4.3	63	1013	W	3	0	C.	4	Sunny
2	T	8.2	3.9	6.8	5.0	70	1020	W	3	1	Cu.	0.5	Bright
3	Wed	9.2	4.6	9.2	8.2	86	1023	SW	3	8	Sc.	1.5	Cloudy
4	Th	11.4	8.0	9.2	7.8	86	1007	SW	3	8	Sc.	1	Showers

Date: Jan 2007   **Weather Data Collection Sheet**   **Place** Tamworth, UK

Make your own weather data collection sheet. Here is an example that you can copy and use if you like. You can easily produce data collection sheets if you have a computer.

THE BEAUFORT SCALE

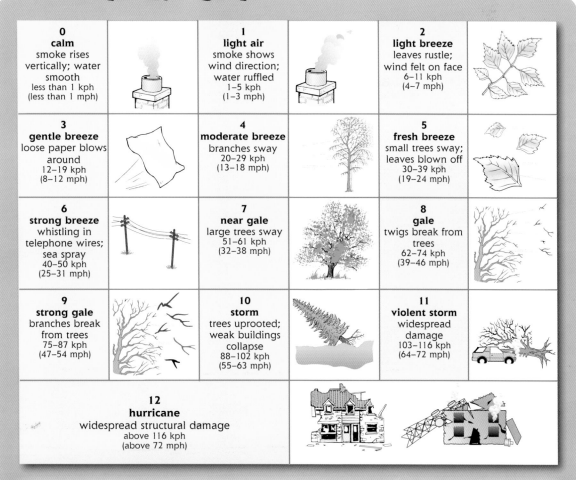

These drawings help to work out the wind's strength according to the Beaufort scale. Look around you and decide which one is right for the wind you can feel. The wind speeds are in kilometres per hour (miles per hour).

Graphs and charts using ICT

Collecting **data** would be a waste of time if it were never looked at again. Using ICT (Information and Communication Technology) means that you can spot patterns in the weather more easily. You can type in data, edit it, and print out copies. Data can be sent to others via e-mail. It can also be put onto web pages so that people around the world can look at it.

Like a professional **meteorologist**, you can use a spreadsheet to create graphs from the data. Choose the type of graph carefully. For rainfall, use a bar chart to make it easy to see which day had most rain, least rain, or the same rain as another day. For temperature, use a line graph to show temperature increasing and decreasing. A pie chart can show which wind direction was most common.

Using a computer to record and analyse your weather data means that you can find out what information the data contains.

TRY THIS YOURSELF!

Use a spreadsheet to make these calculations.
- Finding totals – for example, how much rain has fallen.
- Finding the sum – for example, how many days the wind blew from each direction.
- Finding averages – for example, the average dry temperature.
- Finding maximum and minimum temperatures.

You can also fill in your data sheet by hand. Then use a calculator to do the calculations.

Finding errors

If you put two or more sets of data into a graph, it will help show if you have made any mistakes. Wet and dry temperatures could be graphed together. If the **wet temperature** is higher than the **dry temperature**, then data has been recorded or entered incorrectly. Maximum and minimum temperatures can be recorded on the same graph. If the minimum temperature goes above the maximum, something has gone wrong!

Once you have a spreadsheet with its graphs, the file can be saved and reused month by month. Each month, type in the data and resave it using a sensible new file name to help identify it.

Professional **meteorologists** have special **software** packages to help them present their reports to the media. These packages can arrange weather icons on maps, and can include charts to explain the changes in the weather.

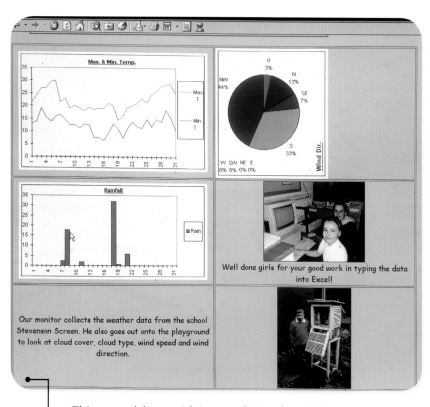

Well done girls for your good work in typing the data into Excel!

Our monitor collects the weather data from the school Stevenson Screen. He also goes out onto the playground to look at cloud cover, cloud type, wind speed and wind direction.

This spreadsheet with its graph is uploaded onto the Internet each month. People around the world can use it to see what the weather is like in Amington Heath, Staffordshire, United Kingdom. You can see the latest version at www. amingtonheath.staffs.sch.uk/data6.htm.

Ideas for forecasting weather

Any amateur **meteorologist** would like to predict what sort of weather is coming. This is not a simple task! Professional weather forecasters are quite good at making short-term forecasts. However, they use very sophisticated **data** collecting devices, and powerful computers. When it comes to long-term forecasts, they are still not very successful. This is especially the case when the forecast is needed for a small area. Local weather forecasters may be more accurate!

Everybody wants to know if it will rain. This is not easy to predict, but there are some pointers that will help to decide if there is going to be **precipitation**. Try using the chart below. This chart refers to low level clouds only. It also requires readings from a **barometer**.

Will it rain?
Start on the left and work across choosing the best descriptions

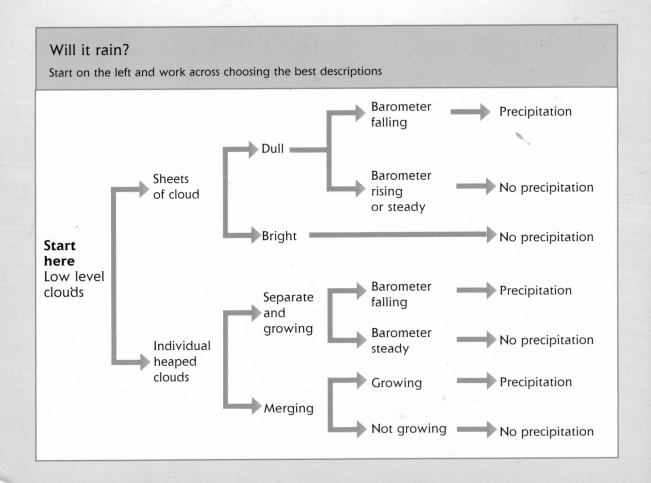

Making your own predictions

If you want to make your own weather predictions, then you need to think about the things that will help you collect the right data. The chart below shows some of the factors that you must consider.

You can predict the temperature overnight, to tell whether there will be a frost or not. The temperature usually falls at a steady rate at night time. This means that you can predict what the lowest temperature will be. Read the temperature at dusk and then an hour and a half later. Make a graph showing the temperatures and hours until dawn. Draw a straight line joining the two temperature readings. Continue the line and see if it goes below zero before dawn.

Keep good records of what weather you predict. Write down what you thought would happen and compare it with what did happen. Good ideas can be used again and those that did not work can be changed.

Things to consider when predicting the weather			
Time of day	Midnight	Dawn	Midday	Dusk
Season	Winter	Spring	Summer	Autumn
Temperature	Very cold	Cold	Warm	Hot
Air pressure	Very low	Low	High	Very high
Air pressure trend	Steady	Falling	Rising	Erratic
Wind strength	Calm	Light	High	Very high
Wind direction	North	East	South	West
Humidity	Low	Medium	High	Very high
Cloud amount	Clear (0 **oktas**)	¼ of sky (2 oktas)	½ of sky (4 oktas)	Full sky (8 oktas)
Cloud type	**Cirriform** (feathered clouds)	**Cumuliform** (heaped clouds)	**Stratiform** (layered clouds)	Giant clouds
Precipitation	None	Drizzle	Rain	Snow

Making a local weather forecast

Weather can be a very local event. It sometimes rains at the front of a house and is quite dry at the back! The better you know your local area, the more likely it is that you will be able to predict what will happen to the weather there. If you live near water, there will be a lot more moisture in the **atmosphere.** You could find out more about this by keeping a record of wind direction and rainfall. You should soon be able to tell which winds bring wet weather to your area, and which bring dry weather.

The best weather prediction is to say that the weather tomorrow will be the same as it was today. There is a seven in ten chance that you will be right!

Where you live

The geographical situation of your region will influence the type of weather you should expect. If you live more than 48 kilometres (30 miles) from the coast, then you will not have sea showers or sea breezes. Even quite small hills in the local area will produce different kinds of weather. The **windward** side will receive more **precipitation** than the **leeward** side.

The chart below shows some ways in which the place you are in can affect the weather. The date and time can also make a difference to the weather you can expect. The chart will not help you to predict the weather on a specific day, but will give you some things to think about, especially when you visit different places.

Ways in which the place you are in can affect the weather					
Location / Time	Seaside	Inland	By water	Mountain	Valleys
Day	Sea breeze	Warm	Cool	Cool	Warm
Night	Land breeze	Cool	Fog	Frost	Fog
Winter	Storms	Cold	Cool/**lake effect**	Very cold	Cool
Summer	Breezes	Hot	Warm/showers	Cool	Warm

TRY THIS YOURSELF!

Predict whether a **cumulonimbus** cloud will bring a storm.

- Is it raining heavily?
- Is there falling **air pressure**?
- Is the wind getting stronger?
- Is the **humidity** rising?
- Is there a giant cloud with an **anvil** head at the top?
- If the answer to all those questions is yes, then it is likely that a storm is approaching.

When a cumulonimbus cloud approaches, it's time to go indoors and watch the rain pour down. You may also hear thunder and see lightning. It may even bring hail with it.

Weather sayings

For thousands of years, people have relied on farmers to provide food. For most of that time, there were no professional weather forecasts. As farming is dependent on the weather, people used sayings to pass on ideas about forecasting the weather. However, people did not keep records of the success of these sayings, so some may be more useful than others.

Different meanings

Some weather sayings have more than one meaning. Perhaps people from different areas interpreted them differently. Some sayings are not very reliable.

"Cows lie down before rain."
Some people believe that if cows lie down, then it is going to rain soon. Others believe that if cows lie down, then it is a sign of good weather. It is obviously not a very trustworthy saying!

Is this cow lying down because rain is coming, or because it is going to be hot? Cows probably do not take much notice of the showers, and are not a very good guide to the weather!

However, there are some interesting sayings about the weather and forecasts that have some truth in them. Here are some of them:

"Rain before seven, fine before eleven."
Rain brought by a **frontal system** often lasts less than four hours as it passes overhead. This saying is good for a forecast at any time, not just before 7:00 a.m.!

"Red sky at night, shepherd's delight,
Red sky in the morning, shepherd's warning."
Red skies in the evening are caused by dust in the dry western sky. This means there are no clouds to bring rain. If there is a red eastern sky in the morning with layered clouds being lit up by the Sun, it can mean that the dry weather has passed and there may be some rain on the way.

"Mackerel sky, mackerel sky, never long wet, never long dry."
A **mackerel** sky has a sheet of clouds in rounded heaps. This means that rain will arrive sometime between six hours and three days later. Generally, if the mackerel sky appears suddenly out of a clear blue sky, the rain will arrive sooner rather than later.

*It is not surprising that a weather saying was based on this beautiful sky. Red sky at night only works for the northern **hemisphere**, where weather generally moves from west to east.*

Professional weather forecasts

The radio, television, newspapers, and the Internet all give us lots of **data** and information about the weather.

To make use of professional forecasts, you need to know roughly where you live on a map of your country. Your own location will not always be marked on the map, so you must look for the cities that are nearest to you to help work out exactly where your area is. You will need to know what the symbols that **meteorologists** use mean. These are usually easy to understand. They represent cloud, **precipitation**, temperature, and wind and **air pressure**.

In detailed television forecasts, two types of weather maps are usually used. The first are large-scale maps of an area with lines called **isobars** showing air pressure and how the weather is moving. The second kind of map has symbols that are rather like pictures to show details of wind, precipitation, and temperature. Television and radio forecasts are also used to give warnings about severe weather.

Television weather reporters provide useful weather data in a way that can be easily understood. The presenter describes the weather situation and points to the symbols to help explain the situation. The presenter also gives forecasts showing how the weather will change over the next day or so.

The weather reports in newspapers also use symbols that are easy to understand. They often include statistics about the region, country, and world. They also give details of indexes relevant to the country, such as the **Heat Index (HI)**. This shows how hot it feels according to temperature and **humidity**.

For very up-to-date weather information, the Internet is useful. You can find out about current weather and forecasts in almost every place in the world.

Forecasts for weather at sea

Weather forecasts apply to the seas as well as the land. The seas are divided into areas so that ships can listen out for the weather forecast for where they are. These shipping forecasts are read out on the radio at the same times each day. Details are always read in the same order so that people at sea will know which information is coming next.

These symbols are like those used on weather maps on television and in newspapers. They vary in style, but all give the same basic information.

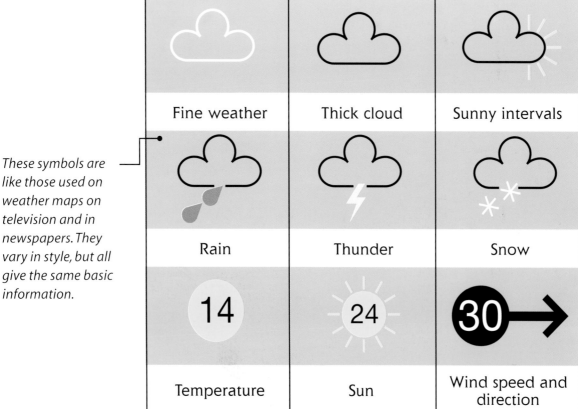

Fine weather	Thick cloud	Sunny intervals
Rain	Thunder	Snow
Temperature	Sun	Wind speed and direction

How the professionals do it

Weather watchers work together a lot. Every day, thousands of weather stations around the world share their **data**. This means that it is almost possible to show what the whole world's weather is like.

The idea of sharing weather data has developed over the years. At the Great Exhibition of 1851, held at Crystal Palace, London, UK, daily weather reports were displayed for the public to read. In the 1850s, the British government founded the first proper Meteorological Department. When the first forecasts were given to the public, there was much discussion about how accurate they were.

Mathematical weather forecasts

Early weather forecasters thought that the Earth could be divided up into sections, and that observations could be made in each section. These observations could then be made into a set of numbers, which would give a weather forecast. In 1922, Lewis Richardson published this idea in his book, *Weather Prediction by Numerical Process*. He imagined that thousands of mathematicians could be used to work out a forecast. His idea had to wait until the invention of high-speed computers in the 1950s.

The Great Exhibition of 1851 helped countries to exchange ideas and inventions. In 1861, Admiral FitzRoy, the first head of the Meteorological Department, helped to bring about one of the first public weather forecasts.

The idea of predicting the weather is very complicated. The amount of data needed is huge, as there are so many things that affect the weather. The most powerful weather computers in the world work round the clock in Washington D.C., USA, and Exeter, UK. The data collected from round the world is turned into digital data that can be processed by these computers.

Once the data is processed, experienced **meteorologists** do the final work on the forecast. They have the latest data from **satellites**, and can spot any errors made by the computer. While the forecasts are being completed, the next batch of data is already being processed.

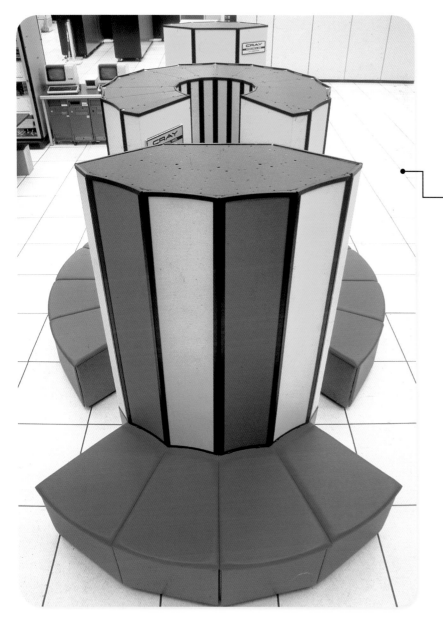

The enormous computers needed to process weather data are far too big to sit on a desk! They need a special room to themselves. Work is going on constantly to improve the computer programs that produce weather forecasts.

Finding out about weather round the world

Before the 1800s, famous people like Thomas Jefferson, George Washington, and Benjamin Franklin were keen weather watchers. They encouraged other people to be interested in the weather.

In the 1830s, Samuel Morse invented one of the first fast communication services, the telegraph system. It meant that people could exchange weather **data** much more quickly. By 1849, daily weather maps were displayed in the **Smithsonian Institution** in the United States. After ships were lost in storms in the Crimean War (1853–56), the British government set up the English National Weather Service in 1854. The American service was set up after storms in the Great Lakes in 1868 and 1869. By 1873, an international meteorological organisation was established, and in 1950, the present World Meteorological Organisation was founded. Today, this organisation helps thousands of people and governments to measure the weather. They try to turn weather data into a pattern of weather predictions for the whole world.

*This **satellite** image shows the white swirls of the clouds above the Earth. It can be put onto the Internet very soon after it is received from the satellite.*

Weather satellites

A lot of data comes from satellites orbiting about 36,000 km (22,000 miles) above the Earth. A series of five satellites can cover the middle section of the Earth. They produce pictures of the part of the Earth they can see. The other satellites used are the polar-orbiting satellites. These travel round the Earth at a height of about 900 km (560 miles). They can only see a section of the Earth at a time, but they see it in greater detail. They usually cross the equator about fifteen times a day on their orbits.

Satellites produce lots of pictures. Some show data as colour-coded pictures. The images may be used to show thickness of clouds, temperature or the height of waves. These complicated images help **meteorologists**, but are not so easy for the general public to understand. Other satellite images can be understood by everybody. Many universities and government groups display these more simple, up-to-date weather images on the Internet. These can now be used by weather enthusiasts as well as professional weather reporters.

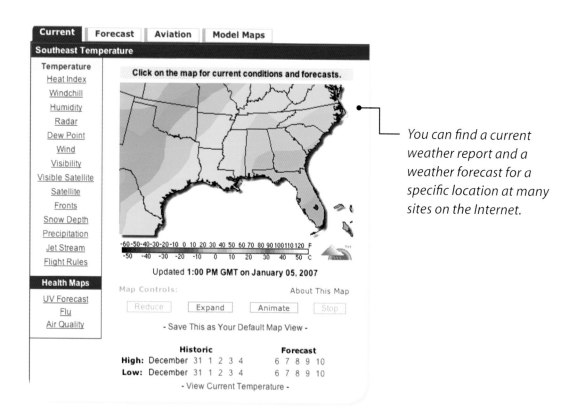

You can find a current weather report and a weather forecast for a specific location at many sites on the Internet.

Photographing the weather

If you are interested in the weather, why not take photographs of interesting weather conditions? Don't worry if some of your photographs don't come out very well – photographing the weather can be difficult.

Whenever you are photographing the weather, you must follow a very important rule. Never look directly at the Sun or point your camera at the Sun. You will damage your eyesight.

The type of camera you use will make a difference to your final picture. The more sophisticated the camera the better the pictures are likely to be. Don't be put off if you have a basic camera, it will still give interesting results. If you don't have a camera, you can buy a disposable camera cheaply which will give you a chance to capture observations. If you are trying to photograph colours in the sky, they may not turn out as you expect. Don't be disappointed, keep trying and you will have many successes. Record the key facts alongside the photographs. Arranging them in an album will make them more interesting. You could sort them in the order you took them, or by theme (for example the different cloud types).

The patterns and textures in the weather can be very attractive. Frost (shown here) and dew can make stunning subjects for photography.

Digital pictures

If you have a digital camera, you can take photographs and see what they look like without having to get them processed. It is possible to take a photograph, see what it looks like, and then retake it if necessary. You can also edit the images, and change their colours and brightness in an **ICT** package. Digital images can easily be built into presentations or **animations**. For example, an image of the same cloud can be taken every few minutes. These can then be displayed quickly one after another, showing the changes in the cloud's shape. This animation will look similar to a video clip. Digital images can easily be displayed on websites.

TRY THIS YOURSELF!

Use a notebook to record the key facts about each picture you take:

- What was photographed
- Where it was taken
- When it was taken (the date and time)
- Why you thought it was interesting
- What camera settings, filters or lenses were used

These photographs were taken at regular intervals, and could be made into an animation to show the movement or formation of clouds.

Record-breaking weather

Many people are interested in records and record-breaking events. Weather records can be very interesting. Can you remember the hottest day in your area? The table below compares **data** from towns and cities called Tamworth. Remember that a day that is hot for Tamworth in the United Kingdom could be thought of as a quite cool day for the people of Tamworth, Australia!

Why do you think that people are so interested in record breakers?

Weather data for the warmest months in each location				
	Average high temperature	Average low temperature	Average precipitation	Month
Tamworth, NSW, Australia	32.0 °C (89.6 °F)	17.0 °C (62.6 °F)	92.5 mm (3.6 inches)	January
Tamworth, Staffordshire, UK	22.0 °C (71.6 °F)	12.4 °C (54.3 °F)	56.0 mm (2.2 inches)	July
Tamworth, New Hampshire, USA	12.4 °C (54.3 °F)	6.2 °C (43.2 °F)	185.9 mm (7.3 inches)	July
Tamworth, Virginia, USA	31.6 °C (88.9 °F)	18.4 °C (65.1 °F)	115.5 mm (4.5 inches)	July

This data uses the nearest available weather data for each place. Not all of the weather stations are official sites. The data collected was in different units of measurement. These had to be converted so that they could be compared. To compare summer temperatures in the two **hemispheres**, different months had to be used for the data.

. Tamworth, UK
·Tamworth, NH, USA
· Tamworth, Virginia, USA

Tamworth, NSW, Australia ·

The four towns around the world called Tamworth have very different weather. It is better to compare their averages – their usual weather – than simply saying which one is hottest or wettest and looking at their extreme weather. You will then find out more about the weather conditions in these places.

One of the best ways of finding out current records is by looking on the **Internet.** Remember to check very carefully exactly what the record claims. Use your knowledge to work out what the records mean. Are the 'record breakers' telling the whole story? Are they claiming a world record, or one just for their area? You never know – if you measure the weather, one day you might measure a record!

WORLD RECORDS

Records are good fun, but they say more about the unusual than the usual. Here are some extreme world records:

- Highest world temperature: 58°C in Al Azizia, Libya on 13 September 1922.
- Lowest world temperature: -89.2°C in Vostok, Antarctica on 21 July 1983.
- Highest world annual total rainfall: 26,461 millimetres in Cherrapunji, India during August 1860 to July 1861.
- Highest world daily rainfall: 1870 millimetres in Cilaos, La Reunion, on 15–16 March 1952.

The places holding the world records for the highest and the lowest ever recorded temperatures are never likely to have similar weather to each other!

Glossary

air pressure pressure, at the surface of the Earth, caused by the weight of the air in the atmosphere

animations series of drawn images displayed quickly one after the other to give the impression of a moving picture.

anvil iron block on which smiths hammer metal into shape. In this book, it is part of a cloud that is this shape.

atmosphere gases that surround the Earth

barometer instrument for measuring air pressure. It may also show whether air pressure is rising or falling.

Beaufort scale system of recording wind speed, devised by Francis Beaufort in 1805. It is a numerical scale ranging from 0 (calm) to 12 (hurricane).

bulb rounded end of the glass tube of a thermometer, containing the liquid

cirriform highest form of clouds made up of ice crystals in thin feather-like shapes.

cumuliform a type of cloud consisting of rounded heaps and a darker, flat base

cumulonimbus cumulus cloud of great height. It often gives showers of rain or is a sign of approaching thunderstorms.

data facts that can be investigated to get information

dry temperature current air temperature. Use with the wet temperature to work out how much moisture is in the air.

evaporation process by which a liquid turns into a gas. In the weather, it usually refers to water turning into water vapour.

frontal system forward facing edge between two air masses of different density and temperature

Heat Index (HI) a method of calculating how hot it feels according to temperature and humidity

hemisphere half of a sphere. In geography, the world is split into two halves – the northern and southern hemispheres.

humidity measurement of how much water vapour is in the air

hygrometer instrument for working out relative humidity

isobar curved line on a weather map linking points of equal air pressure

lake effect weather effect which causes large amounts of precipitation to fall on places near lakes or other large areas of water

leeward direction towards which the wind blows

mackerel type of fish. In weather terms, a "mackerel" sky is made up of lots of clouds that look like the pattern on a mackerel's back.

meteorologist a person who studies the weather by gathering and analysing data

oktas eighths of the sky

precipitation moisture that falls from clouds in a variety of forms, for example rain, snow or hail

relative humidity meteorologists' term for humidity, usually given as a percentage.

satellite device made to orbit the Earth, receiving and transmitting information

Smithsonian Institution series of museums and galleries in the United States.

software computer programs

stratiform layered clouds

weather vane piece of apparatus with a pointer that shows the direction that the wind is coming from. It is labelled with the points of the compass.

weather station collection of weather instruments that measure the weather regularly.

wet temperature temperature read with a special thermometer that is kept wet by a wick. The reading is used to work out the amount of water in the air.

wick specially woven piece of cloth that draws up a liquid

windward side the wind blows from

Find out more

Re-read the weather sayings on pages 18 and 19. Can you think of an experiment to try out one of the sayings to see if it works? How will you make your experiment scientific? You will need several observations.

How successful are the professionals? Keep a record of the forecasts for your area and check to see what proportion are correct. Which sorts of weather do they find hardest to predict? Is it true that in seven out of ten days the weather will be the same as the day before?

If you have a barometer, try out the 'Will it rain?' chart on page 14. Does it help predict **precipitation**?

Websites

http://maps.google.co.uk/maps
Use a website such as Google Maps to see where the oceans are in relation to your location. This will help to give you an idea of the weather brought to your area by different winds. It will also help you to locate your area on the weather maps on TV and on the Internet.

http://www.bbc.co.uk/schools/whatisweather/
What is weather? from the BBC will give you a lot to think about. Try the different links to find out all about the different types of weather.

http://www.amingtonheath.staffs.sch.uk/intro.html
The Staffordshire School Weather Data Site has good ideas for collecting data and for setting up your own weather station. You can also follow a link to help you graph your data.

More books to read

Instant Weather Forecasting, Alan Watts
   (Adlard Coles Nautical, 2004)
Eyewitness Weather, Brian Cosgrove
   (DK Publishing Incorporated, 2000)
Discovering Geography: Weather, Rebecca Hunter
   (Raintree, 2003)

Index